AF428465

GRIGOR TATEVATSI (medical, grammatical, and legal questions), SAYINGS 1346-1409

Susanna Grigoryan

Title: GRIGOR TATEVATSI (medical, grammatical, and legal questions), SAYINGS 1346-1409

ISBN: 979-8-89248-422-0

Author: Susanna Grigoryan

Cover image: Personal Image

Publisher: Generis Publishing
Online orders: www.generis-publishing.com
Contact email: info@generis-publishing.com

CONTENT

FOREWORD

In the 5-th century translation of the Bible in armenian became a powerful impetus for the development of various types of spiritual activity and interpretative literature in particular. Almost simultaneously with the translation, literature interpreting the Bible arose, forming the principles of understanding the Holy Book.

Grigor Tatevatsi (1346–1409) is one of the most famous medieval Armenian interpreters of the Bible. He has 32 works, among which the most famous is **"Book of Questions",** which is a complete and comprehensive interpretation of the Bible.

Grigor Tatevatsi is one of the most famous theologians of his time, master teacher, who has many kinds of questions in his works including grammatical ones.

The book presents some medical, jurisprudential and grammatical questions of Tatevatsi, which are extremely interesting as the views of a 14th-15th century thinker.

About two dozen of Tatevatsi's many sayings are also presented, which will represent the universal thoughts of the medieval Armenian thinker.

MEDICAL TERMS IN THE LITERARY LEGACY
OF GRIGOR TATEVATSI

The rich literary legacy of Grigor Tatevatsi gives u good reason to find him as a great philosopher, theologian, economist, teacher, interpreter of "art writing", grammatist, speaker and fabulist. To all these we can implicitly add an outstanding theorist of medicine as well. In his creative legacy the medical problems include more than two hundred pages and there are more than two hundred terms related to this field. It' s worthy of note the fact of anatomical, physiological and human organ's detailed description. Above mentioned is to prove, that he was the great expert of this sphere of medicine too.

About seventy years ago, in 1946, an extremely remarkable work was published. "L. A. Oganesyan, History of Medicine in Armenia, Part two, Yerevan 1946", where there is also a reference to Grigor Tatevatsi's medical views. In a few pages, at a proper scientific level, the author presents the medical questions found in Grigor Tatevatsi's literary heritage, and one can only be surprised that no professional monograph on this subject has been written so far.

The medical questions and analyses separated by us only from Grigor Tatevatsi's "Book of Questions" exceed several dozens of pages, that is, if we combine the rest of the medical questions found in Tatevatsi's literary heritage, and compare them with other medieval authors, we can definitely speak of Grigor Tatevatsi's systematized medical views. Let's say more; we are dealing with an interesting Senior Doctor who remains in the shadows, and the answers to many of his questions are confirmed by the data of modern medicine. And is he really Senior Doctor? We think, yes, because no other medieval author has covered such a variety of issues, such comprehensive analyses.

The titles of the chapters and so-called "praks" (i.e. sections, subsections) of his works confirm the fact that he was rather advanced in medicine.

What is an illness?

An illness and treatment.

Why are the kidneys covered in fat, but the heart and liver are not?

About the stomach.

A question about sputum.

Why is the same water sweet in the mouth, salty in the eye, smelly in the nose, and bitter in the ear?

Why is a human's right side stronger than the left one?

How many joints and bones are there in the human's body?

About tendons and bones.

A question about people's colors.

Why don't Tatars have beards?

The questions about the human body composition, and in particular, the chapter "A Question on Fortune Telling with Facial Features", are interesting; on the one hand, the author, according to the ancient philosophers, pays attention to the connection between body and temperament, but on the other hand, he expresses open-mindedness and warns that they should not be accepted as absolute truth, but nevertheless advises to take into account that the nature suggests something there.

"...Such signs do not force a person to do anything, but show the inclination [according to the nature] of that object" (Grigor Tatevatsi, Book of Questions,

Constantinople, 1729, p. 246. hereinafter - Book of Questions). There is also the fact that a person can improve his/her temperament with intelligence; "and they are able to prevent them with mind if they want... to restrain the actions of these signs by fasting, prayer and controlling the body", therefore: "... one cannot judge a person according to these signs" (ibid.). And in this sense, the reference to Plato in this passage becomes only a confirmation of the above-mentioned warning. "And Plato says, if a person has a resemblance to an animal, he/she shows a corresponding behavior" (ibid.), testifying that Tatevatsi was well acquainted with Armenian and foreign authors in any field.

According to the semantic fields, the terms and concepts were divided into three groups.

1. diseases, medicine, treatment (used concepts: doctor, healer, hospital, treatable, incurable, help pain, health, well-being, long-lived, short-lived, get sick, illness, severe disease, disease, body infection, pestilential and unclean air, air pollution, unhealthy food, bad food, night food, eye pain, blind, go blind, madness, headache, closed ulcer, stomach disease, rotten tooth, catch strep throat, sore throat, leprosy, scabies, sick parent – sick-born son (in case of an hereditary illness), follow fasting, fasting, chewing finely, rinsing, squeezing, preparing medicine for the patient, remedy and pharmacies, ointment, grass flowers, roots, leaves, fruit, wormwood water, pig's milk, dog excrement, lily water) .

2. state of mind, temperament (used concepts: temperament, pride, envy, gluttony, lust, anger, laziness, greed, cheerful, angry, brave, timid, fearless, cunning, shy, foxy, lustful, decent)

3. body composition, anatomy (used concepts. internal major organs: heart, brain, liver, lung, spleen, kidneys, bile. internal organs: uterus, joints, bones, tendons, main tendon, stomach (pulling, gathering, digesting and expelling - features of the stomach), qalasike* (upper vein of the liver). external organs: doors: eye, ear, nostril, mouth. navel, breast, urethra. anus. other external organs: head, pelvis, throat, navel, belly, skin, flesh, blood, senses, veins, hair.

lymph, blood. bile black and white bile, saliva.

to become blood-containing, temperature and dryness of the heart, to promote, to conceive, pregnancy, menstruation, hereditary features of parents.

Among these, the word "latrine" is attested as "exit (in the sense of toilet)" in the Grabarian sources. Tatevatsi uses it in the row called "doors" in the sense of "anus"; "aghvesabaro (foxy, fox-like)" is one of his neologisms; "qalasike" is not attested in the dictionaries, either.

General questions on theory

In general, Tatevatsi believes that illness is the lack of health, as darkness is the lack of light, and death is the lack of life: "...**kindness is ability, and evil is lack of it like darkness as a lack of light, and sickness as a lack of health, and like death as a lack of life**" (Book of Questions, p. 16): And in general, one can say that the medical views of the author are a continuation of his philosophical views. "**Human life is nothing but walking to death,**" he writes (Grigor Tatevatsi, Book of Sermons called Winter Volume, Constantinople, 1740, p. 328. henceforth Book of Sermons, Winter): In this case, the patient's task should naturally be to fill in the deficiency.

According to Tatevatsi, the key to longevity and healthy living is to eat moderately and eat less meat; disease, according to him, is largely connected with eating, therefore health is connected with fasting; at the beginning people "did not eat meat or drink wine, but only ate fruit, so they were very long-lived, but then, when they began to use more bread, meat and wine, they became short-lived, and they will continue to live shorter because of eating too much. ... A human's illness comes with eating... then health is kept with fasting", and diseases caused by eating at night kill more people than the sword of a war "eating at night kills more people than the sword of a war" (Book of Sermons, Winter, p. 130).

It is clear from his review that our ancestors kept sheep to get wool for clothing and not for food; cattle meat was used for eating. ("And now we keep sheep for clothing, and oxen for food, donkeys for carrying loads, horses for mounting, dogs for chasing the enemy, hawks for catching birds, etc.'' (Book of Questions, p. 217):

The more a person neglects to keep his health, the closer he gets to illness, and the complete absence of health turns into its opposite, that is, there is no life, and there is no illness either. "And know this too, the more health decreases, the more disease increases. the more the body weakens, the more decaying increases, and if health decreases at all, the disease disappears as well" (Book of Sermons, Winter, p. 22).

In fact, many diseases are evidenced by the existence of various medical remedies: medicines, plasters, herbs, their roots, fruit. "The abundance of medicinal drugs and plasters, flowers and roots, leaves and fruit of various medicinal plants indicate the abundance of diseases in the body" (Book of Questions, p. 531).

Obviously, Tatevatsi's questions and analyses bring forth a main topic around which his reflections go round. The goal of his questions is the human perfection (and not only in this field), so his opinion about the man of the future is also predictable. To the question of what the man of the future should be like, this Christian teacher's answer, of course, was expected to be in accordance with biblical standards. However, Tatevatsi's combination was unexpected; the man of the future is free from all defects, whether spiritual or physical. He will be healthy, like Moses the Prophet, whose tooth did not move in his old age. handsome as Absalom, swift as Asaiel, strong as Samson, long-lived as Methuselah, rich as Solomon, honorable as Joseph, beloved as Jonathan, free as Augustus; Here the whole section is cited: "Because [the man of the future] will have Body Beauty, Speed, Strength, Freedom, Will, Health, and Immortality. And his soul will have Wisdom, Love, Unity, Power, Honor, Fun and Joy. And although all these are more than the glory of the present man of the earth, let's give an explanation with some examples. It would please you if you were as beautiful as Absalom, without any failures; or if you were a swift runner, like Asaiel, who reached the goats; or if you were as strong as Samson, who killed a thousand people with the jaws of a donkey; or if you were free like Augustus, whom the whole world served; or if you were like

Solomon, whose all heartfelt desires became true; or if you were healthy like Moses, whose eye sight did not fail, nor did his tooth move; or if you were long-lived like Methuselah who lived a thousand years. And even if one of all of these were given, [a man] would like to exchange it for his kingdom, and if all these given together, it would be the supreme enjoyment of the world.

And let us add to all these the wisdom of Solomon, the like of which was not found elsewhere on earth; or the friendship of David and Jonathan, who loved each other as much as their souls; or the unity of the apostles, who were like one heart and one person; or the rule of Alexander [the Macedonian] who conquered Asia, Europe, Libya; or if you were honored like Joseph, whom the Egyptians worshiped as a god; or if you were carefree like Enoch and Elijah, who were not afraid of death or anything else; or if you were as happy as if someone condemned to be hanged gets a kingdom, as they say about Saul: he lost a donkey, and he found a kingdom" (Book of Questions, pp. 761-762).

1. diseases, medicine, treatment Tatevatsi gives four causes of diseases. the first reason is natural, which occurs due to the lack of necessary means or polluted air. "And the disease occurs for four reasons. or due to the lack of necessary means and conditions. or because of the impurity of the air" (Book of Questions, p. 665). In this case, he recommends to be treated with medicines. "If a disease is a violation of nature, it should be treated with medical drugs" (ibid.). So, the treatment of the other three types of diseases is in the hands of the patient: to eliminate the crime, to come to justice, to self-regulate, medical drugs have nothing to do here ("The second ones are those who do not repent of sin, God gives them sickness for conversion. The third type of sickness is given to the chosen best ones, whose recovery is the shame of evil, as in the case of Job. Fourth sickness type is given by fate to people, so that they do not become proud, like the case of the apostle Paul, and so that people do not allow deviations from nature" (ibid.)). "And if it is another disease, you must examine yourself to see if you have done bad deeds, if your honesty is lacking, restore it, and then there will be healing of body and soul from God and not with drugs".

In general, he views illness as an intermediate state between life and death, "One must also know that illness is an intermediate state between life and death." (ibid.).

He urges the patient to consult a doctor on time. One that has a serious illness should visit the doctor quickly and undergo an examination, otherwise the doctor will not be able to help after death" (Book of Sermons, Summer, p. 320). A patient is closest to the illness like a child to the childhood, or an elderly man to the old age. "When you are sick, you are close to your illness, when you are a child, you are close to your childhood, and when you are old, you are close to old age" (Book of Sermons, Winter, p. 37). He warns that as health gradually declines, the disease gets worse with it at the same time. "When the health decreases, the disease appears, when the body decreases, decaying appears" (Book of Sermons, Winter, p. 22).

We all know how important the cleanliness of the environment is for civilized people today, but it is surprising that it was also important in the 14th-15th centuries. Tatevatsi mentions not only food but also polluted air as a cause of diseases. "Doctors say that pestilential and polluted air is more harmful than bad food. Bad food goes to the stomach but does not reach the heart, and the smell goes directly to the heart and harms a person the most." (Book of Sermons, Summer, p. 514).

More than once, Tatevatsi emphasizes the role of a skillful doctor and draws a parallel between a bad priest and an ignorant doctor. A wise doctor first treats the cause of the disease. "A wise doctor first removes the cause of the disease, then cures you with medicines" (Book of Sermons, Summer, p. 145). A faithful doctor first tastes the medicine himself. "Honest doctors first try the medicine themselves, then give it to the patient" (Book of Questions, p. 316). A wise doctor does not give the medicine too early or too late. "...a doctor should not give the medicine before or after the pain, but at the right time to get well, otherwise it will be useless and harmful" (Book of Questions, p. 467). "If someone has a headache, but the doctor heals the leg, then the doctor is a fool, because one puts a plaster on the painful place," he writes about unwise treatment (Book of Sermons, Summer, p. 191). A careful doctor not only cures, but also follows up on the patient's future condition. "If a doctor gives a medicine to the patient today, he must ask about the patient's well-being tomorrow" (Book of Questions, p. 680).

A stupid priest is considered similar to a venipuncture [doctor], who, along with bleeding, also cuts the tendon of the patient and causes many injuries (Book of Sermons, Summer, p. 320).

Among the diseases, he talks about ulcers, sore throats, eye pain, gout, toothache, the answer to each of which is medicine. "Medicine is the answer to a disease" (Book of Sermons, Winter, p. 15). There are also incurable diseases, for example, leprosy and scabies.

"A covered ulcer will not heal without the doctor's medicine" (Book of Sermons, Summer, p. 309).

"Just as plaster and medicine cure an ulcer, so confession cleanses sins and heals the soul" (Book of Sermons, Summer, p. 309).

"...A rotten tooth is removed so that others do not become infected" (Book of Sermons, Summer, p. 310).

"The dust that fills the eyes little by little eventually blinds" (Book of Sermons, Summer, p. 563).

"What is the medicine for a sudden sore throat [we are talking about boghmai disease]?" Doctors say they carefully take blood from the jugular vein and then give Salsola water to rinse.

Or they mix pig's milk, dog excrement and lily water, which helps with sore throat" (Book of Sermons, Summer, p. 264).

"Sixthly, leprosy and scabies are incurable" (Book of Questions, p. 371).

Questions asked in favor of complex treatment do not go unnoticed; in particular, it is necessary to know that the feeling of pain comes from the head. "Pains and contractions of the body come from the head" (Book of Sermons, Winter, p. 196). If you have stomachache, it is recommended to fast. "...When the stomach hurts, they fast, because the cause of stomachache is overeating" (Book of Sermons, Winter, p. 126), and he generally advises to "eat little by little and with satisfaction, but not in large pieces like a beast" (Book of Sermons, Summer, p. 348).

In case of eye pain, he recommends covering with a black cloth. "The sages say that the color black collects and strengthens vision, therefore, when the eye hurts, black cloth is tied to the eye" (Book of Sermons, Winter, p. 382).

He refers to the healing features of snake venom. "And although the poison of the serpent's venom is deadly, yet the dead snake, when burned, becomes a powerful antidote" (Book of Sermons, Winter, p. 138).

He talks about the heredity of some diseases. "There is no doubt that during conception, the diseases and colors of the parents are mixed together in the menstrual zone, just as Adam gave birth to a son with sorrow, like a parent who brought pain into the world gave birth to a son who was born with pain" (Book of Questions, p. 439), "At the moment of conception, the child is born with the color of the element that dominates at that moment." (ibid., p. 245), although he also records that a parent with a defect can have a healthy child. "An imperfect father can give birth to a perfect son, just as a sighted child is born from a blind man" (Book of Sermons, Summer, p. 67).

Probably, free hospitals existed in medieval Armenia. "...Doctors of the hospital receive the payment of the patient's medicines from the king and not from the patient," testifies Tatevatsi in the Winter volume of the Book of Sermons (Book of Sermons, Winter, p. 299).

2. State of mind, temperament. The seven biblical sins became a topic of discussion for any medieval author, perhaps only because they were almost impossible to avoid. Tatevatsi often examines them in order to see the human more perfect and healthier. He considers two of them - pride and envy - as disorders of mental development. "Some consider gluttony and lust to be carnal desires, while others consider them mental. And I say two out of seven - pride and envy - are simple mental sins, pride coming from knowledge, and envy from desire" (Book of Questions, p. 559); two of them are physical, and the remaining three are both mental and physical; " And I say two out of seven - pride and envy - are simple mental sins, pride coming from knowledge, and envy from desire" (ibid.). The most serious sin of these, according to Tatevatsi, is pride [arrogance], because according to him, if other diseases are noticeable by their characters, pride remains covered at all, "**All unhealthy things are made known to us by a tangible proofs, as theft by a stolen item, fornication by lust, but pride is [dangerous] because it does not show itself by a tangible feature**" (Book of Questions, p. 562).

The fact that these are diseases and can be overcome is beyond doubt for the author. a sinner with sorrow may seek recovery as a sick person from a disease; "Sinning with sorrow is a sickness and a temptation, and the sick person hastens to recover, and a tempted person seeks finding a sinless path" (Book of Questions, p. 33).

And only a stupid person will not fight leaving the desease by itself. "Only a foolish patient will say: I will eat and drink, no matter I will get well or I will die" (Book of Questions, pp. 18-19). According to Tatevatsi, a gluttonous person is like a patient who steals water ("He is like a patient who steals water: the more he drinks, the more thirsty he gets" (Book of Questions, p. 570), the solution of which is also treatment.

Suffering from mental illnesses, for example, from diabolism, doesn't allow to get married. "...There are many marriage bans, such as spiritual or non-spiritual kinship, imperfection of nature, being a harlot, madness, being a servant [in that house], or forced marriage; in these cases, they can be divorced" (Book of Questions, p. 610).

He also talks about the danger of laziness, which leads to sadness and inactivity. "There are two types of laziness: one who turns away from spiritual goodness and prays with difficulty, etc. this is called sorrow" (Book of Questions, p. 559).

In the chapter "Questions about facial features"... people are funny, angry, brave, coward, brave, cunning, shy, foxy, harlot, decent, etc.

According to the author, a person matures not only physiologically, but also mentally; one reaches perfection at the age of fifty. "Fifty-year-old age is a jubilee and freedom that gets you rid of love for the material world and turns you toward God" (Book of Questions, p. 378).

It should also be noted that Tatevatsi often summarizes his thoughts with set phrases. For example, he ends his discussions about a gluttonous person as follows: "such a person is hungry after eating and thirsty after drinking" (Book of Sermons, Summer, p. 262). His message about eating right also gets the value of a set expression, "...eat your food like a medicine" (ibid.).

3. body composition, anatomy: The sections related to body composition and anatomy are very large. Tatevatsi makes both internal and external organs the subject for discussion. He considers the heart, brain, liver, lung, spleen, kidneys, gall bladder to be the main human organs, because if the rest of the organs are damaged, a person can stay alive, but if these main organs become damaged, it leads to death. **"If a person's eye, ear, hand, leg are damaged, the person lives, but if the main organs are damaged, a person dies"** (Book of Questions, p. 241).

("And the main organs are **the heart, the brain, the liver, the lung, the spleen, the kidneys, and the gall bladder**." (Book of Questions, p. 241).

"He calls the eye, ear, nostril, mouth, navel, breast, urethra, and anus 'the doors of the body'" (Book of Questions, p. 241).

The stomach regulates digestion by its pulling, gathering, digesting and expelling functions.

The liver regulates blood circulation with 438 vessels. (Book of Questions, p. 244). The upper vein of the liver is called "qalasike*". (Book of Questions, p. 244). The liver is the start point of blood vessels. 438 veins start from the liver.

He describes in detail human bones, tendons, veins, lymph, and blood.

The description of the embryo and pregnancy is quite interesting; according to Tatevatsi, the embryo breathes on the fortieth day; the heart is formed first; and umbilical cord feeding begins on the seventh day, "And on the seventh day, the embryo begins to draw blood from the mother's womb through the navel, like a pumpkin or a watermelon draws juice from its stem." (Book of Questions, p. 261) "And the first of all the organs, the heart develops, because the heat of the seed is gathe red in it" (ibid.).

Of course, the discussion on whether the questions asked more than six hundred years ago are correct or incorrect is beyond our material, especially since Tatevatsi himself considered wisdom much higher than health as the supreme gift of God. "The wise people say that the greatest gift from God to a human is wisdom, which is greater than life and health and wealth" (Book of Questions, p. 178). However, one thing is indisputable that due to Tatevatsi, we had a outstanding theoretician of medicine in the 14th-15th centuries. No one can deny that Grigor Tatevatsi has systematized medical views waiting for being studied, and let's sum up our attempt to present these views with a set expression from the summer volume of his Sermons Book, and the first part of this expression undoubtedly refers to Grigor Tatevatsi himself. "The wise say: He who knows medicine is a doctor, but he who knows justice is not always just " (Grigor Tatevatsi, Book of Sermons called Summer Volume, Constantinople, 1741, p. 76).

We believe that this article, being put into circulation for the first time, can bring a serious addition to the medieval Armenian medical study.

List of concepts

(English and Armenian transcription)

air pollution-stahakuthyun odoc

anger-barkutyun

angry-barkacox

a rotten tooth-phteal atam

belly-por

bile-palgham, maxdzn

black bile-sev maxdzqn

blind-koyr

blood-aryun

body-marmin

bones-woskerq

brain-uxex

breast-stinq

catch strep throat-zphoxsn brnel

covered ulcer-xoc tsackeal

disease – akht

ear – akanj

eat little by little-manr-manr tsaskel

eye- achq

eye pain, sore eye- achqacav

expelling-vtarakan

decent-parkesht

digesting-haloxakan

disease- hivandutyun

doctors-bjishkq

fasting-pahq

fat-charp

fruit-ptuxq

grass flowers-caxiks xoto

go blind-kuranal

hair-mazn

head- glukh

headache-glxacav

healer-heqim

health-aroxjutyun

heart-sirt

help pain-ognel cavin

hospital-hivandatun

incurable- anbujn

infect, spoil – varakel

infection-apakanutyun

internal major organs-nerqin glxavor andamqs

joints-zoduvacq

kidneys-yerikamunq

latrine/anus/-artaqnoc, hetancq

laziness-tsulutyun

leaves-terevs

leprosy-yerqunot

lily water-zjur shushanin

liver-leard

long-lived-yerkarakeac

lung-thoq

lust-bxjakhohutyun

lustful-gijaser

lymph-hyuthq

madness -ajsaharutjun

main tendon-glkhavor jilq

menstruation-dashtan

mouth-beran

nape-tsotsorak

night meal, eating at night-gisherajin kerakur

navel-portn

nostril-pinchq

ointment-mlham

remedy and pharmacies- spexaniq ev dex bjshkakanq

roots-armtiq

pestilential and unclean air-odn jantahot ev xarnak

pharmacies- dexq bjshkakanq

pig's milk-zkathn xozin

pregnancy-hxacumn

prepare medicine for the patient-arnel zdexs hivandac

pulling-qharshoxakan

qalasike-qalasike

rethra-jrhexn (mizancq

rinse-voxoxel

saliva-xux

scabies-snqnotn

senses, sense organs-zgajaranq

severe disease-canr hivandutyun

short-lived-karchakeac

skin-morth

sore throat- boghmai

spleen-phaycexn

squeeze-kxkxel

stomach-stamoqs

stomach disease-hivandutyun stamoqac

temperament-xarnuacq

temperament-dzgtumn bnutyean (xarnuacq)

temperature and dryness of the heart-srtin jermutyun ev chorutun

throat-xrchaphox

treatable-bujeli

to conceive-bexmnavoril

to draw blood- aryunacuc linel

to follow fasting-pharriz arnel

to get sick-hivandanal

to promote-barexarnel

unhealthy food-tchar kerakur

unhealthy food-vat kerakurn

upper vein-verin erak

veins-yerak

venipuncture-yerakahat

well-being-woxjutyun

white bile-xarteash maxdz

womb-argand

wormwood water-zoshnarin jurn

LEGAL CONCEPTS IN
GRIGOR TATEVATSI'S "BOOK OF QUESTIONS"

Key words – Rulebook, judgement book, right, law, investigation, rule, custom.

In 1964 was published "Armenian Law Book", which brought together the generally recognized legal acts of medieval legal thought.This is a brief analysis of medieval legal thought, there is no reference to Grigor Tatevatsi (who lived in the 14th-15th centuries), because he did not create a separate work dedicated to legal regulations. However, there are so many legal questions and analyzes in his numerous works that if we bring them together, we will certainly have a unique work of the great thinker of the time comprehensively referring to the legal relations of the period. For example, in the Summer volume of "Book of Sermons", Tatevatsi writes: "And the one who gives an early and sloppy report... first he shows his light-mindedness and secondly, that he is a briber."

As a rule, the researchers in the field of law mention several sources of Armenian legal thought: customary law, church rules, borrowed laws, national judgement books, bibliographic works. In the sense of sources, the legal concepts of Grigor Tatevatsi's "Book of Questions", as well as other works, are information extracted from bibliographic works. However, his questions are from customary law, from national judgement books and even more from church rules.

Legal concepts are found much more often in Grigor Tatevatsi's "Book of Questions" and Sermon Books. Let us say, for example, that the word "law" alone is used by the author more than three hundred times in the "Book of Questions" in the sense in which it is found in the Rulebook or Judgement Books, canonical documents and bibliography.

Comparing the 288 rules included in the fifty-seven chapters of the "Book of Armenian Rules" with the questions of Grigor Tatevatsi's "Book of Questions" (as well as the sermons of the Summer and Winter volumes of "The Book of Sermons"), as we said, Grigor Tatevatsi addressed many of them.

According to the author, the concepts of "law", "order", "rule", "right" are distinguished as follows: "The law and the order come from above"[1]: "And the right is the execution of the examination and its fair compensation[2]: "... the law is a rule and a limit for those who keep and do not keep it." [3]: "...the law is compulsory and the commandment is at will."[4].

The author distinguishes between natural, written and evangelical laws, the purpose of which, in his opinion, is human education.

In general, the legal questions in the "Book of Questions" are about the following main concepts: law, right, judgment, trial, kill, revenge, retribution, custom, repress, disobey, plunder, crime, punishment, penalty, confession, witness, testimony, blasphemy, sin, examine, acquit, repentance, retribution, kontakion, rule . order, will, fear, over tax (coercion), judge, justify, adoption, lawmaker, legislate, legislation.

The crime starts with the smallest, therefore, according to Tatevatsi, a person should be consistent in actions and behavior, the disruption of which eventually leads to a misdemeanor or a more serious sin. "And the forgivable sin is the smallest of us. because after the baptism of my child, first the forgiveness will come, and then the measure of death."[5]. "... it is pride to trample and dishonor the true good. and then we slowly change our mood. and thus perhaps pride is a sin"[6]: "…Seventh, let the cause of the enemy be ours, that he changed to his fault by crossing the command line."[7]:

---

[1] Book of Questions, p. 277:
[2] Book of Questions, p. 384:
[3] Book of Questions, p.340:
[4] Book of Questions, p.340.
[5] Book of Questions, p. 567:
[6] Book of Questions, p. 562:
[7] Book of Questions, p. 277:

n the one hand, he admits that the laws have changed over time, but according to him, there is no doubt that the law establishes the truth. "The other line, because the law was changed according to the advice, but according to the thing it remained forever, because they were the example, but the truth remained."[8]:

It is quite interesting that the author's reference to the restrictive, binding, singular form of laws in the book "On the Ten Laws" is quite interesting. According to him, they are instructions for each person to regulate the relations among themselves by prohibiting, ordering, persuading; "Don't kill. don't lie don't steal do not bear false witness. do not wish. Soka is human and towards a friend and an enemy. Second, there are five commissions and five resignations. Third, it is five minor. and five negatives. Fourth, there are five commandments. and the five prohibitions"[9].

Tatevatsi is absolutely convinced that the society needs to have laws, a court, and investigators. Speaking about fatalism and making a reservation that if its supporters are right, the author writes that in that case there would be no tax: "no right to judgment and investigation and no political law and no proper retribution to the good and the bad, because the tax was a tyrannical act." . honor and punishment were on the floor and not on the person."[10]: Let's notice that in these few lines, the author used at least seven legal concepts, which are quite close to the modern understanding of these concepts. law, judgement, trial, law, retribution, repress, punishment.

Undoubtedly, in addition to being valuable source information, Tatevatsi's questions and analyzes are also very remarkable in terms of the testimony of a contemporary, to what extent this or that regulation of law was preserved in his days.

Comparing these concepts with the current RA Criminal Code, at least six articles of the Code reflect the author's definitions in one way or another. Tatevatsi talks about a fair judgment, coercion and appropriateness of punishment, which are

---

[8] Book of Questions, p 369:
[9] Book of Questions, p 340:
[10] Book of Questions, p 12:

presented in the main requirements of the relevant articles of the RA Criminal Code. The requirement of judicial fairness is governed by Articles 61, 336 and 352 ("just punishment", "unjust sentence"). the appropriateness of punishment under articles 48, 49, and coercion under article 45 ("It is not considered a crime to cause ... damage under the influence of coercion")[11].

Conclusion - Thus, bringing together the jurisprudential concepts found in the "Book of Questions", we can state that although the author does not have a separate work on that field, his questions are very interesting and diverse. On the one hand, Tatevatsi was conservative in them and tried to explain the approaches of his ancestors without going beyond the canonical definitions, on the other hand, based on the problems of his time, he interpreted them in a new way.

Reference list

1. Grigor Tatevatsi, Book of Questions, Constantinople. 1729.

2. Grigor Tatevatsi, Summer Book of Sermons, K. Polis, 1741.

3. Rulebook of Armenians. A, work.V. Hakobyani, Yerevan, USSR State Publishing House, 1964.

4. Criminal Code of the Republic of Armenia, Yerevan, 2021.

---

[11] Criminal Code of the Republic of Armenia, Yerevan, 2021.

MEANING MOVEMENTS OF LEGAL CONCEPTS (NARROWING, EXPANSION OR INDIVIDUAL APPLICATION) IN THE WORKS OF GRIGOR TATEVATSI

Some legal concepts, as evidenced by the early grabar (ancient Armenian), later appeared with shifts in meaning, narrowing or expanding, often also moving away from the original meaning, as we have in the case of the word "ojit" ("dowry"), which originally meant a gift brought by the bridegroom to the bride, and later he became an inheritance from his father's house, brought by the bride. We fixed the author's new use of the word GITHWORN (githwor, Guilty), since the grabar (ancient Armenian) dictionaries do not testify, and Grachya Acharyan in "Armenian root dictionary" mentions only the use of Grigor Tatevatsi in the ". According to the author, the word "apaharzan" is a legal concept that has lost its force in its time.

Key words – Judgement book, legal act, order, inheritance law, mandatory-prohibitive orders, dowry (ojit), share of paternal property (bajinq).

Grigor Tatevatsi's works and analyzes in addition to being valuable source information, are also very remarkable in terms of the testimony of a contemporary, to what extent this or that regulation of law was preserved in his days.

In the article, we tried to analyze the applications some of legal concepts in the works of Grigor Tatevatsi the differences in semantic applications compared to the Old armenian (grabar) word forms, the narrowing and expansion of the word meaning. We have tried to pay special attention to those idioms, which in this or that dialect appeared by narrowing or expanding the meaning of the word, or have original author's usage.

We have examined the word «օժիտ» (ojit) "dowry" from customary law (here, in the sense of inheritance law).

One of the famous armenologists of the time, Nicholas Adontz, in his work **"Armenia in the age of Justinian"**[4: 208], examined in detail the problem of state, legal regulation of marital relations in medieval Armenia and made interesting remarks, particularly regarding customary law. Referring to the short stories published by Justinian "On the Inheritance Law of Armenians", one of which declares that Armenian women are deprived of inheritance rights, he writes: "The presence of the word **«օձիտ» (ojit) "dowry"** in grabar (Old armenian) in the sense of the **bride's share** makes Justinian's claims that Armenian women married without **dowry** extremely doubtful. The mentioned word belongs to non-Aryan elements of the Armenian language, that's why its antiquity is beyond doubt" [4: 216]. Then in the footnote, he adds fleetingly: "It is possible that the word **«օձիտ» (ojit. "dowry")** is also used in Armenian in the sense of the gift that the groom gives to the bride, as in Assyrian [4: 217] ".

Adontz's not so convincing conclusion is confirmed by the following testimony of Grigor Tatevatsi. In the "Summer volume of "Book of Sermons" he writes: "Three things should be given to the bride. i.e. share, dowry and gifts: (բաժինք, օձիտ եւ պարգեւք - bajinq. ojit. pargevq): the share was given for wedding expenses by father, the dowry was given by the groom, and the gifts were given by the relatives" [2: 203]. So the dowry (օձիտ, ojit) was given by the groom, from the bride's father's house was called a share, which was inferior in volume and weight to the dowry, because it was intended to cover the wedding expenses, then all three gifts were presented to the bride, i.e. the future housewife. In any case, it is beyond doubt that in the 14-th and 15-th centuries, when Grigor Tatevatsi lived, the dowry continued to exist as a gift given by the groom to the bride. In the Bible [3:…] we find this word used in this sense several times.

Thus, by combining the facts, we can talk about the word "ojit" ("dowry") as a native armenian word. It was originally called the gift that the groom gave to the bride. It was probably much moreweighty than the share given by the girl's father, because firstly, the share was given to cover the wedding expenses and secondly. Later, when the «օժիտ» (ojit) "dowry" by the groom had already stopped, it took the place of "the share" as a name, almost pushing the latter out of use. In modern Armenian, բաժինք "bazhink" in its original meaning, that is, in terms of the income given by the girl's father, has been preserved in the Karabakh-Goris dialect in the forms "pezhink, pazhink" (պէժինք, պաժինք) [5: ...].

In another case, talking about the divorce, (ապահարզան, apaharzan) in the chapter "What Was the Writing of Divorce?" (ապահարզան. apaharzan) in "Book of Questions", the author the author gives a historical explanation, because in his opinion the divorce was caused by certain circumstances.

Asks a question: "why did the Mosaic Law allow divorce", but the New Law did not? The answer is related to another question asked later: "how should the marriage be performed? ". "The idea here is that the bride and groom should see and like each other by heart and will before the marriage, and then get married" [1: 610]. Here, in fact, we have the predominance of a pre-made choice, which presumably, according to the author, would not lead to divorce, and according to Tatevatsi, the Mosaic Law was to prevent murder: "Moses gave the right for the spouses to give each other a divorce letter. And this was because of their cruelty; so that there should be no murder" [1: 400]. as according to that logic, if the principle of own will was not kept from the beginning, then forcing an incompatible couple to live together would probably lead to the above-mentioned crime under certain circumstances.

In other words, according to the author, the word "unmarried" (apaharzan) is a no longer valid legal concept.

He ordered six cities to be sheltered and given to priests: three in the land of Canaan, three beyond the Jordan. And 42 from other surrounding areas, making 48. So that those committing involuntary manslaughter may be freed while the priest is alive. And when the priest dies, they should go to their places... And still the Georgian nation keeps this, because the sinner is freed by entering the church [1: 392]. (translait by Susanna Grigoryan).

We have a new word GITHWORN ("githwor". Guilty), because the Old armenian dictionaries do not testify, and the only dictionary, Hrachya Acharyan's "Armenian Root Dictionary", only testifies to the author's use of Grigor Tatevatsi. Acharyan refers to the word under the article «Գայթ» GAYT, referring to Grigor Tatevatsi and the Amaran volume of "Book of Sermons " and "Book of Questions", that is, there is no doubt that the only source of this word is Grigor Tatevatsi.

The testimony is interesting to the extent that it refers to one of the circumstances of the crime in the Middle Ages. it refers to the formed city-shelters, where the apparent criminal (in this case, the unwitting criminal) was able to avoid responsibility, and as Tatevatsi testifies, in Georgian reality, that function was performed by the church.

A city of refuges mentioned in the Bible, so that those who committed an involuntary murder, sheltering inside city, could avoid punishment; According to the author, the church performed this function at least in the 14th century in Georgia.

Cities of refuge, mentioned in the Bible, so that those who committed an involuntary murder, sheltering inside the city, could escape punishment; According to the author, (that is, at least as early as the 14th century) in Georgia, the church performed this function.

Reference

1. Grigor Tatevatsi, Book of Questions. Constantinople, 1729.

2. Grigor Tatevatsi, Book of Sermons: Summer Volume, Constantinople, 1741.

3. Bible. Saint Petersburg, 1817.

4. Nikolas Adontz. Armenia in the Period of Justinian, Yerevan, 1987.

5. A.Yu.Sargsyan. Karabakh dialect dictionary, Yerevan, 2013.

SEMANTIC AND OPERATIONAL EXAMINATION OF A NUMBER OF TERM WORDS OF GRIGOR TATEVATSI

In the article, we set the task of conducting a semantic study of Grigor Tatevatsi's terms and characterizing their operational use. In particular, we examined how the author's works use concepts expressing legal prohibition.

Translation of the Bible into Armenian in the 5th century became a powerful impetus for the development of various types of spiritual activity. Almost at the same time with the translation, literature interpreting the Bible arose, forming the principles of understanding the Holy Book. Grigor Tatevatsi is one of the most famous theologians of his time, a teacher and church leader, a student of Hovhannes Vorotnetsi, the founder of Tatev University, from 1390 he himself became the rector of this famous educational institution, establishments. Tatevatsi in all his works referred to most of the 288 provisions of the Armenian Canonical Book. His analyzes also include numerous grammatical issues.

Key words – Canonical Book, legal prohibition, wedding prohibition, prohibition on the ordination of priests, mandatory prohibitive instructions, grammatical inhibitory particle.

In the 5th century translation of the Bible in armenian became a powerful impetus for the development of various types of spiritual activity and interpretative literature in particular. Almost at the same time with the translation, literature interpreting the Bible arose, forming the principles of understanding the Holy Book, canonized by three Ecumenical Councils (Nicaea, Constantinople and Ephesus) and the Holy Fathers, passing them on from generation to generation.

History of the question – Historical events dictated to bring together the great Armenian Catholicos Hovhan Odznetsi (8th century), and also to supplement the canons based on the Bible, national traditions and customs and create the Armenian Canon Book.

Grigor Tatevatsi (1346 – 1409) in all his works referred to most of the 288 regulations in the Armenian Canon Book (Ruleook), who is one of the most famous theologians of his time, master teacher, who also has many grammatical questions in his works.

Vazgen Hakobyan, who worked out the Armenian Rulebook, writes in the preface of the book: "Among the jurisprudential monuments created by the Armenian people in the Middle Ages, the Rulebook is the only one that acts, in a certain sense, as an official collection of legal acts that have been generally recognized over the centuries. Neither Mkhitar Gosh's, nor Smbat Gundstable's judgement books are official legal acts. They are works of great thinkers of the time"[12].

Appropriately evaluating the Rulebook and at the same time even not considering the judgement books of Mkhitar Gosh and Smbat Gundstable as official legal acts, nevertheless, the author considers the latter "works of great thinkers of the time". We think, that the historical role Mkhitar Gosh's "Judgement Book" is recorded not only for Armenian society, but since the 19th century, foreign researchers have considered it one of the sources of European legal thought (see Ferdinand Bischoff's "Das alte Recht der Armenier in Polen" and "Das alte Recht der Armenier in Lemberg" ("Armenian Old Law in Poland" and "Armenian Old Law in Lemberg")[13].

---

[12] A, worked out by Hakobyan V., (1964), **Rulebook of Armenians,** Publishing House of the Academy of Sciences of the Armenian SSR, Yerevan, p. XVI.

[13] **Ferdinand Bischoff,** (1857), Das alte Recht der Armenier in Polen, Wien, **Ferdinand Bischoff,** Das alte Recht der Armenier in Lemberg, Wien, 1862.

We already meet a significant part of modern Armenian legal concepts in these works.

The semantic and operational examination of Grigor Tatevatsi's terminological words shows that since Tatevatsi himself referred to most of the rules of the Armenian Canon Book., and therefore he also examined the legal concepts and legal prohibitions used in them.

In the article, we aimed to conduct a semantic examination of Grigor Tatevatsi's term words and give a description of their operational use. In particular, we examined how the concepts expressing the legal ban used in the author's works.

For example, in the Armenian Rulebook, which are also thoroughly analyzed by Grigor Tatevatsi: "One should pray facing east", "Gospel reading order", "On Pentecost and Ascension", "About baptizing a child", "Women should not go on the stage", "What part of the earth was allotted to each of the apostles?", "On readmission of a person who has confessed his guilt", "On staying firm and faithful to the Nikiou Creed", "On the dismissal of Nestor's followers... ", "About sorcerers, witches, conjurers... ", "On the Order of the Religious", "About empty-talkers and pranksters", "How to finish the fasting with cheese, fish, eggs, wine", "How to keep the 40 days of Vardavar", "That the leprous and scabby cannot be religious", "One must say "Holy God" and then "Crucified", contain many clauses expressing legal prohibition and concepts.

Perhaps only in terms of Shahapivan's rules, which are the only ones in the Rulebook that provide for corporal punishment, Grigor Tatevatsi has no questions.

Almost in all modern countries, appropriate legal norms are defined, in case of violation of which one or another restrictions or punishments apply. These restrictions are regulated as a legal prohibition, for example, in the Republic of Armenia by a number of codes and government decisions. In particular, the RA government's decision No. 685 of 2019 approved a list of physical defects and diseases as an obstacle to the appointment of a judge, including blindness, muteness, deafness. Decision No. 98 of 2019 established a larger list of obstacles to public service, including "schizophrenia" and even "mood disorders", "mental and behavioral disorders"[14].

In Armenian written monuments, the legal prohibition originally operates within the framework of the ten commandments of the Bible. It is grammatically formed by the inhibitory particle "mi" (не, don't) (մի՛ սպանիր – не убивай, don't kill].

Further additions that go beyond the commandments retain their logic, for example, a ban on coronation or priestly ordination is formalized in criteria, the violation of which would lead to undesirable consequences within the commandments.

As we mentioned, grammatically, these prohibitions continue to be formed by the inhibitory particle "mi", in the singular. And the Grigor Tatevatsi's answer to the question, why mandatory-prohibitive orders are formulated in singular, they are almost no different from the principles that are applied in the modern court system; "Why does the law say it in singular and in the one and the same person: do not commit murder, etc. First of all, so that everyone considers himself relevant and does not get lazy, saying that it is said in general. Secondly, a person that keeps the law is more honorable to God than the whole world, that is why he speaks in singular"[15], that is, everyone considers that all commandments are addressed to him and are not general words that can be followed or not followed.

Undoubtedly, in addition to being valuable source information, Tatevatsi's questions and analyzes are also very remarkable in terms of the testimony of a contemporary, to what extent this or that regulation of law was preserved in his days

---

[14] **Grigor Tatevatsi**, (1729), Book of Questions. Constantinople, p. 340..
[15] **Grigor Tatevatsi**, Book of Questions., p. 610.

and what concepts were used. We bring the author's analysis about the prohibition of the crown.

In the case of the crown the legal prohibition is formed by the following concepts!

– spiritual or physical kinship.

– weakness of nature

– prostitution

– this situation

– the service

– by violence, in which case dissolution of marriage was allowed.

In context, the above words were concepts that constituted the legal prohibition of the crown in the Middle Ages.

A number of diseases or circumstances could become the reason for the prohibition of the crown, which in this context again acquires the value of a legal concept, moreover, in the presence of these, the separation of a married couple became possible "... because there are many restrictions on the crown. as the kinship is spiritual or physical. or weakness of nature. or prostitution. or this situation. or the service. or by violence. or some other such reason. with which they separated the man and the woman[16]".

Tatevatsi considers the couple's consent necessary. "If the two wills are not equal and harmonious, the marriage is unstable, whether forced or involuntary action. And consent is visible when the eyes see and the tongue approves"[17]. According to him, the meaning of this is that before the marriage, the consent of the couples should precede. "This is a recommendation that the bride and groom should

---

[16] **Grigor Tatevatsi,** (1741.) Book of Sermons: Summer Volume, Constantinople, p. 199:
[17] **Grigor Tatevatsi**, Book of Questions., p. 610.

see the marriage before the crown and the love of the heart and the will and then the crown"[18].

Tatevatsi has interesting questions regarding the legal prohibition when examining the right to practice as a priest, especially since new words are used when listing the features characterizing the prohibition. They are: «այլամազ» – ailamaz, «տրեալ» – treal, «քածավարին» – qatsavarin (all of which according to the explanation of the root mean «կնաբարո» – "cnabaro", that is having the behavior of a woman, not characteristic of a man).

We bring the author's part: "First, the blind (կոյրն - kuyrn).... Secondly, the bekealn (բեկեալն – desponded in good actions. Thirdly, լեզուատն (lezuat - the mute). Fourth, մարմառոտն (marmarotn – having a ulcerated skin, if the skin is torn and sore). Fifth, քոսն (qos – scabies). Sixth, երքունոտն. սնքնոտն – erqunotn, snqnotn – skin diseases). Seventh, քածավարին, այլամազն (the khatsavarin, ajlamazn – that is having the behavior of a woman). Eighth, թաղամսաւորն (thaghamsavorn – the stratified skin). Ninth, ականջատն – (akanjatn – the one without ears), Tenth, կրճատ. (krchatn – is the circumcised one. Third, մայլեալն, տրեալն (malealn, trealn – that is having the behavior of a woman, not characteristic of a man. The twenty, փոշտանկն (phoshtankn - who have hernia).

Add to these the sick (հիվանդն - hivand) and the crazy (գիժն – gijn). It is not acceptable that the mind is obsessive and the sin is sick".

In essence, the part contains a list of prohibitions for priestly work (which refers to the old liturgy), according to which the blind, the mute, scabies, the stratified skin, the the sick etc, in essence, the part contains a list of prohibitions for priestly work, according to which the blind, the mute, scabies, the stratified skin, the the sick etc.

***

¹⁸ **Grigor Tatevatsi**, Book of Questions., p. 371:

As we mentioned, grammatically, these prohibitions continue to be formed by the inhibitory particle "mi'", in the singular. In the case of a legal prohibition on priestcraft, Tatevatsi uses the negative particle "not" – *ոչ* (voch) («*ոչ է ընդունելի*» – "not acceptable").

Thus, the semantic and operational examination of Grigor Tatevatsi's terminological words shows that since Tatevatsi himself referred to most of the rules of the Armenian Canon Book, he referred to the legal concepts and legal prohibitions used in them, and when examining the legal prohibition of crowning and ordaining a priest, he applied new legal concepts.

Reference

1. Grigor Tatevatsi, (1729), Book of Questions. Constantinople.

2. Grigor Tatevatsi, (1741) Book of Sermons: Summer Volume, Constantinople.

3. A, worked out by V. Hakobyan, (1964), Rulebook of Armenians Yerevan, Publishing House of the Academy of Sciences of the Armenian SSR,

4. Criminal Code of the Republic of Armenia, (2021), Yerevan.

5. Ferdinand Bischoff, (1857), Das alte Recht der Armenier in Polen, Wien, (1862) Das alte Recht der Armenier in Lemberg.

SAYINGS OF GRIGOR TATEVATSI

Do not fill your transitory life with laziness and inaction, but do good.

*

*   *

Medicine is the answer to disease.

*

*   *

Table and food are more honorable when hungry than full.

*

*   *

The habit of eating at night kills more people than the sword of war.

*

*   *

He who falls into the sea cannot see the waves, but one at the shore sees the waves.

*

*   *

Human life is nothing but a process towards death.

*

*   *

Life is a city with two doors, we enter through one and exit through the other.

*

*   *

No matter how long a person lives, two days are his: birth and death.

*

*   *

Wisdom is the firm foundation, and works are the superstructure. A house without a foundation is made of sand.

*

*   *

The wise say: He who knows medicine is a doctor, he who knows justice is not always just.

*

*   *

It is a human habit to make what exists to be like what is imagined in the mind.

*

*   *

In nature, love comes first, then wisdom.

*

*   *

Emptiness is the mother of all sins.

*

*   *

A deceiver is a deceiver of God.

*

*   *

Extreme wealth and poverty equally harm a person.

Perfect love has no fear.

*

*   *

He who closes his eyes does not face the light of the sun, but deprives himself of the

light.

*

*   *

A woman is the beauty of the house.

*

*   *

It is easier to tame a beast than to bring an ignorant person to knowledge.

*

*   *

One honorable stone is better than many worthless stones.

*

*   *

An angry person does not see the truth.

*

*   *

What the potter makes will be a pot and not the sky.

*

*   *

One truth does not have to follow many lies.